The science of Fire

LIVING SCIENCE

Rennay Craats

Gareth Stevens Publishing
A WORLD ALMANAC EDUCATION GROUP COMPANY

For a free color catalog describing Gareth Stevens' list of high-quality books and multimedia programs, call 1-800-542-2595 (USA) or 1-800-461-9120 (Canada). Gareth Stevens Publishing's Fax: (414) 225-0377.

Library of Congress Cataloging-in-Publication Data available upon request from publisher. Fax (414) 225-0377 for the attention of the Publishing Records Department.

ISBN 0-8368-2680-9 (lib. bdg.)

This edition first published in 2000 by
Gareth Stevens Publishing
A World Almanac Education Group Company
1555 North RiverCenter Drive, Suite 201
Milwaukee, WI 53212 USA

Project Co-ordinator: Rennay Craats
Series Editor: Celeste Peters
Copy Editor: Heather Kissock
Design: Warren Clark
Cover Design: Lucinda Cage and Terry Paulhus
Layout: Lucinda Cage
Gareth Stevens Editor: Patricia Lantier-Sampon

Every reasonable effort has been made to trace ownership and to obtain permission to reprint copyright material. The publishers would be pleased to have any errors or omissions brought to their attention so that they may be corrected in subsequent printings.

Photograph Credits:
City of Calgary Fire Department: 24 top, 25 right (O. Tveter). Corbis: cover (center), pages 8, 16 bottom, 20 top, 23 top, 25 left. Corel Corporation: pages 5 top, 6 middle, 7 middle, 7 right, 11 middle, 11 bottom, 12 top right, 12 middle, 12 bottom, 13 bottom, 22 top, 22 bottom, 24 bottom, 27, 28 bottom, 31. Digital Stock: pages 6 left, 12 top left, 13 top. EyeWire: pages 10 top left, 17 top, 30. Norm Faulkner, Alberta College of Art and Design: page 23 bottom. Roy McLean: pages 5 bottom, 6 right, 10 bottom left, 11 top left. PhotoDisc: cover (background), pages 7 left, 10 right, 11 top right. Publiphoto: page 29 top (David Nunuk/Science Photo Library). Tom Stack & Associates: pages 4 (Mark Newman), 19 top (Brian Parker), 19 bottom (Spencer Swanger), 26 (Gary Milburn). Visuals Unlimited: pages 16 top (Roger Treadwell), 17 bottom (Jeff J. Daly), 18 (Science VU), 20 bottom (Peter Ziminski), 21 (George Loun), 28 top (Science VU), 29 bottom (Science VU).

Printed in Canada

1 2 3 4 5 6 7 8 9 04 03 02 01 00

Contents

What Do You Know about Fire?

Crackling in a fireplace, fire is beautiful and relaxing. When it burns out of control, however, it can be scary. Although fire is useful, it can also be very destructive.

Fire has fascinated people for thousands of years. It took a long time for people to figure out what fire was, as well as how to make and use it. Fire is still a little mysterious today.

To many people, roasting marshmallows and telling ghost stories around a campfire are family traditions.

Fire plays a big role in our lives. For example, a spark of fire makes car engines run. Fire produces the splashes of color in the sky during fireworks displays. A furnace turns fire into heat when a small jet of gas called the **pilot light** is lit. Natural gas stoves provide flames on which to cook. Fire often makes people's lives easier and more comfortable.

Colorful fireworks help people celebrate events, such as the Fourth of July.

People use natural gas to heat food on a stove. Other natural gas appliances include clothes dryers, barbecue grills, and water heaters.

Puzzler

What breathes, eats, and sleeps but is not alive?

Answer: Fire. It breathes **oxygen**, eats fuel, and can "wake up" and burn again after it has gone out. Read on to discover more about how fire breathes, eats, and sleeps.

Sources of Fire

Many different sources of fire are available today. People create some fires using tools. Other sources of fire occur naturally, without any involvement from people.

Sources of Fire

Lightning	Spark	Friction

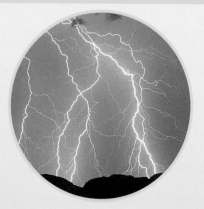

Lightning	Spark	Friction
1. flash strikes objects on the ground	1. two pieces of stone strike together	1. two objects rub together
2. releases 100 million volts of electricity at a temperature of 60,000° F (33,000° C)	2. spark is created	2. temperature rises where they touch
3. sets objects on fire	3. spark sets fire	3. fire starts

Examples

lightning storms that cause forest fires	spark from lighter flint	match striking rough surface

Puzzler

Which sources of fire can people control? Which sources occur naturally?

Answer:
We can start fires using **friction**, chemicals, sparks, or sunshine. We cannot control when or where lightning will strike or when **lava** will **erupt** from a volcano.

Chemicals	Sunlight	Earth's Core

1. certain chemicals mix together	1. shines through glass lens	1. temperature is 9,032° F (5,000° C)
2. create a new chemical and heat	2. lens brings light together to concentrate on one spot	2. heat melts rock near Earth's core
3. heat causes fire	3. temperature rises at spot	3. melted rock escapes to surface through cracks
	4. fire starts	4. sets fire to nearby objects
burning fuel in an automobile engine	sunshine passing through magnifying glass	lava from volcanoes

Fire from the Past

Lightning was our ancestors' main source of fire. They used fires that lightning had started to light fires of their own. One person in the community was in charge of keeping the fire burning. It would be terrible to lose the flame because no one knew when or where lightning would strike again. They even took burning wood from their fires with them when they moved.

Rubbing sticks together creates heat that becomes fire. This method of making fire takes time, patience, and practice.

People eventually discovered how to create fire. They realized that striking certain rocks together made sparks. Then they realized that the sparks started fires if they landed on dry wood or grass. Our ancestors also made fire by rubbing two sticks together quickly. This created friction that made the sticks smoke and burn.

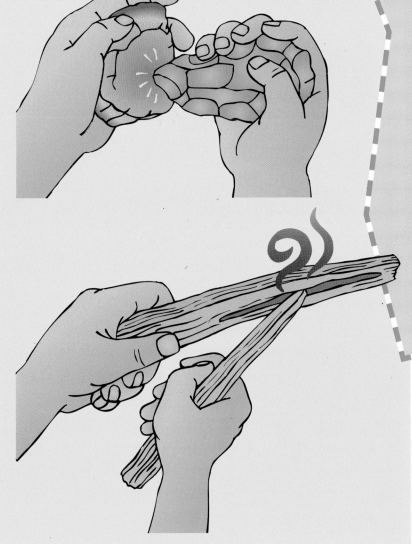

Activity

Creating Friction

Place the palms of your hands together. Rub your hands back and forth quickly while they are pressed together. What do you notice? You have created your own friction! You cannot start a fire in your hands, but they can get very hot.

Fire in Our Lives

Fire serves many purposes and is an important part of our lives. Here are some ways people use fire. Can you think of any more ways that you use fire?

A Gathering Place
is created by fire.
Many families come together around their fireplaces on a cold day. Camping would not be the same without roasting hot dogs or marshmallows and singing around a campfire.

Light from a Fire
can help us find our way in the dark.
Before electric light bulbs were invented, fire and moonlight were the only sources of light at night.

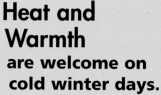

Heat and Warmth
are welcome on cold winter days.
Fire also keeps homes warm. When you turn on your furnace, a spark is created. It **ignites** a flame that heats air. The furnace releases the hot air into the rest of the house.

Power from Engines
starts with fire.
Sparks create a series of explosions inside an **internal combustion engine**, such as the engine in your car. The explosions provide the power that makes the engine run. People have fire to thank for modern transportation!

Activity

Using Fire
Walk through your house and yard with a notepad. Try to find all the items that use fire to work. Write them on your notepad. Your list may include the stove, lamp, furnace, and lawn mower.

Cooking and Baking
require heat.
Our ancestors prepared food over an open fire or inside an oven heated by fire. Modern stoves and ovens that burn natural gas still depend on fire to provide heat.

Kilns Use Fire
to bake pottery.
Wet clay is shaped into pots. The pots are then baked in a kiln at 1,652° F (900° C). The heat makes the pots harden and keep their shape.

A Burning Question

Three ingredients are needed to make fire: oxygen, fuel, and heat. If any of these are missing, a fire cannot start.

Oxygen is easy to find. It is one of the gases in air, and it is all around us.

Wood, leaves, and paper are solid fuels. Oil and gasoline are liquid fuels. Fuel can also be a gas, such as the natural gas that burns in furnaces.

heat

oxygen

fuel

Lightning is a common source of heat for fires. Chain saws and fallen power lines also cause sparks, which provide the heat needed for fire. Heat removes the water from fuel, which allows oxygen to touch the fuel and ignite it.

Solid fuels do not burn well when they are wet. Water keeps oxygen away.

Activity

Ingredients for Fire

Draw a triangle on a piece of paper. Put one of the three ingredients for fire on each side of the triangle. Draw as many examples of these ingredients as you can around the triangle. For example, you could draw an oxygen tank or an outdoor scene to show the oxygen side of the triangle. Use bright colors to make your drawings fiery.

Warming Up to Fire

Fire does not just happen. A heat source must warm the fuel until it catches on fire, or ignites. Heat warms fuel in three main ways.

Convection spreads heat
through the air in a circular motion.

As air heats, it rises. Cooler air moves in below the warmer air. This creates a circular movement of air, called **convection**. The warm air circles and heats the room.

Conduction moves
heat through a material.
For example, a pot handle often becomes hot even though it is not directly over the flame. Heat spreads through the entire pot. **Conduction** does not often start a fire. Instead, it helps spread heat through solid material once a fire has heated a part of the material.

Radiation warms
using heat waves.
If you stand near a campfire or a space heater, you can feel the heat from a distance. This is an example of **radiation**.

Puzzler

Which pot handle would get hotter through conduction— a metal handle or wooden handle?

Answer:
A metal handle would get hotter. Wood does not allow heat to pass through it easily, but metal does. A wooden handle would remain cooler than a metal handle.

Striking a Match

Matchsticks are made from wood or cardboard. To make them burn better, the sticks are dipped in wax. The match tip is made from a chemical that burns easily, such as **phosphorus**. Safety matches usually have a red substance covering the tip. The red part does not catch on fire. This prevents the matches from catching on fire if they rub together in the matchbox.

Various types of matches use different chemicals to create fire.

Matchboxes and matchbooks have a strip of rough material on them. When you strike a match against this surface, friction rubs away some of the match's red part and creates heat. The exposed phosphorus tip underneath catches on fire. The fire burns from the tip of the match down to the wood or cardboard.

A matchbook is a safety device. It prevents matches inside from lighting until someone strikes them against the rough surface on the cover.

Wooden matches are often called "strike-anywhere" matches. Almost any rough surface will cause the match to light.

Forest Fires

Lightning is a common cause of forest fires. Lightning is very hot when it strikes the ground. Its heat can set trees or grass on fire. Wind helps spread fire. A small fire becomes a large, dangerous one in a hurry!

Sometimes people accidentally start forest fires. A campfire not put out properly can cause a forest fire. So can a lighted match that is carelessly thrown away. People have to use fire very carefully. Fires can start easily and spread quickly.

Firefighters often dig a fire line around a forest fire. They remove as much fuel from around the fire as possible to try to prevent it from spreading.

Everything looks black and dead after a fire, but forest fires can be good for plants. Fire clears the land so there is space for new plants to grow. The new plants grow well because they are sharing the food in the soil with fewer plants. The burned material also acts as a fertilizer.

New trees grow between burned ones months or years after a forest fire.

Puzzler

How can you be sure that you have put a fire out properly?

Answer: Let the fire start to die down long before you plan to leave. Pour water on the fire and stir the ashes around with a long stick. Add more water and stir again. The coals must be cold and completely wet before the fire is totally out.

Favorable Fire

Sometimes forest fires help the environment. Giant sequoia pine trees grow best in soil that contains ash. Also, some trees need fire to **reproduce**. Lodgepole pine trees are a good example. They will not drop their seeds unless the temperature reaches 113°F (45°C). When a forest fire occurs, the temperature rises and thousands of these seeds are released.

Lodgepole pine seeds are trapped inside a pine cone until a forest fire sets them free.

Farmers sometimes set controlled forest fires. They chop down a forested area and burn the trees. Then they plant their crops in the rich, ashy soil. The farmers use this land until their crops no longer grow well. Then they move to another forested section and plant new trees to grow on the old land.

People who set these fires must be very careful and think of everything before setting the fire. They must never let the fire they set go too far.

Puzzler

What does someone setting a controlled fire need to think about first?

Answer: Which way is the wind blowing? Where will the fire travel? Will people be in its path? How hot is it outside? How wet or dry are the grass and trees? Will they burn slowly or quickly? Where should the fire stop? How will the fire be stopped?

Healthy crops grow on farmland that was once forest. Some crops grow very well in ashy soil.

Fiery Jobs

Fire is used in many jobs. For example, welders use fire to cut pieces of steel and some other metals. Welders also melt pieces of metal together. They hold a flame to the ends and then press the ends together. When the pieces cool, they look like one piece. You may be interested in going to trade school and becoming a welder. Welders help make lots of things, from airplanes to jewelry.

Welders wear a faceplate that has dark glasses built into it to protect their skin and eyes.

Glass blowers use fire to create art. The best way to learn this art is to become an **apprentice** glass blower. You can practice blowing glass with the help of a professional artist. Glass blowers dip a hollow iron pipe into boiling glass. Then they blow into the pipe until the glass bulges into a bulb on the other end. This red-hot bulb is stretched, twirled, and cut to make different shapes. It is held in a fire during shaping to keep it soft. When the glass has the right shape, the glass blower takes the glass off the end of the pipe to cool.

Activity

Do Your Own Research

Have a parent or teacher help you find out about the following careers that involve fire:

- firefighter
- furnace technician
- glass blower
- welder

Glass blowers use fire to heat and shape glass. They create beautiful sculptures in many colors.

Firefighting

Many fires are not controlled. Mistakes, such as leaving a candle burning or overloading electrical outlets, can cause a house fire. When this occurs, people call firefighters to put out the fire. Firefighters also have first aid training, so they can help someone who is injured from fire or smoke.

Firefighters arrive in fire trucks that have long water hoses. The water usually comes from fire hydrants along the street.

Firefighters spray the house with water to put out the fire. A great amount of water flows through the hose. The water pressure is too much for one person to handle, so it takes two or more firefighters to aim the hose.

During training, firefighters learn how fire moves through houses. They understand how fire behaves. They use this information to stop the fire from spreading.

Activity

Rescue Training

Firefighters train to rescue people. They practice carrying dummies while wearing heavy protective clothing. See if you would make a good firefighter. Put on heavy boots, a heavy jacket, and a helmet. Try to drag a 10-pound (4.5-kilogram) object up a flight of stairs.

Firefighters also help rescue people who are trapped in buildings or automobiles.

Firefighters carry oxygen tanks on their backs. The tanks make it possible for them to work near the fire without breathing smoke or gases.

Backdraft

Fire often seems to be alive. It sometimes acts as if it has a mind of its own. Like people, fire needs oxygen to live. It eats fuel, and sometimes it gets sleepy without enough air. A **backdraft** explosion happens when air rushes in and the fire wakes up.

A sleepy fire sometimes gets a sudden air supply and wakes up. An explosive backdraft can happen then.

A fire gets bigger as it burns. The growing fire uses more and more oxygen. At some point, the fire can use up all the oxygen in a room. It then starts to "gasp" for air. The flames get smaller and smaller. The fire goes to sleep, and the room fills with smoke.

If you open a door or window to that room, air enters. The fire wakes up and quickly eats the oxygen in the air. This sucks air into the room so fast the **fire gases** explode. A backdraft explosion is very powerful. It can knock a person all the way across the street.

Activity

Visit a Fire Station
Ask your parents to arrange a trip with you to the local fire station. Ask the firefighters to explain how they fight fires and how they battle backdrafts. Maybe they will even show you a fire engine!

Adding oxygen to a sleeping fire wakes it up. The fire explodes and begins to burn again.

Could Fire Get Higher?

Every day, small rocks fall into Earth's **atmosphere** from space. As they fall, they rub against the air. The friction heats them up and sets them on fire. As they fall to 40–75 miles (65–120 km) above Earth, we can see them as **meteors**, or "shooting stars."

Small particles burn up before they can reach the ground. Some larger particles and rocks survive the fall. These are called **meteorites**.

When meteorites hit Earth, they can create enormous craters in the ground.

Fireballs are very bright meteors that last for several seconds. A tail of flame follows behind a fireball.

The best time to look for meteors and fireballs is during a **meteor shower**. A meteor shower occurs when Earth runs into a cloud of particles in space. Many of these particles enter the atmosphere at once. Sometimes it looks like it is raining meteors!

The meteors in meteor showers all appear to come from one place in the sky.

Fireballs can sometimes be as bright as a full moon in the sky.

Activity

Star Gazing
On a clear night, ask your parents to go outside with you to look up at the sky. Watch for meteors and fireballs. Usually one meteor can be seen every ten or fifteen minutes. During a meteor shower, more than sixty meteors may be visible in one hour.

Fire Safety

Your family can do many things to remain safe from fire. Plan an escape route in case a fire happens in your home. Practice how you would leave your house to escape the fire. Also, check the batteries in your smoke detector. This alarm is an early warning that a fire has started.

Having a fire **extinguisher** in the house is important, too. An extinguisher allows your parents to put out a small fire before it becomes a big one. If you are alone and spot a fire, get out of the house and call 9-1-1, the emergency number. Never try to control a fire yourself. Always tell an adult about a fire and let him or her put it out.

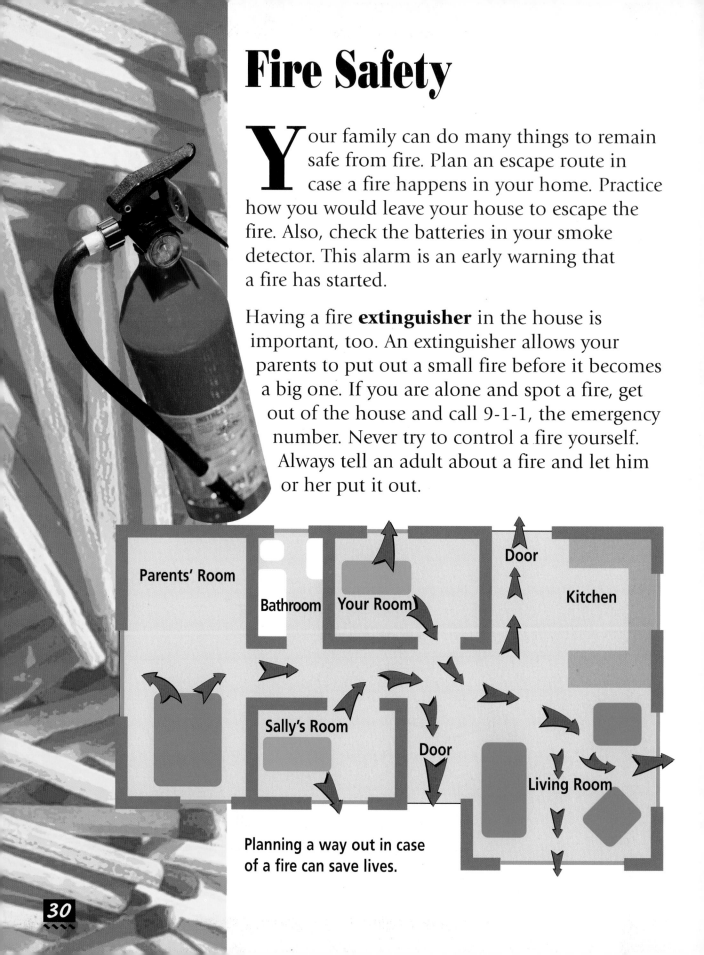

Parents' Room

Bathroom Your Room

Door

Kitchen

Sally's Room

Door

Living Room

Planning a way out in case of a fire can save lives.

Here are some tips to help avoid fires in the first place.

1. Never play with matches. They light easily and can cause a great deal of damage quickly.

2. Make sure fires in fireplaces or firepits are completely out before leaving the area. Check to see if the embers are all cold. If they are not, the fire could heat up and begin burning again.

3. Use candles safely. Only burn them when an adult is with you. Blow out a burning candle before you leave the room. This way the flame cannot cause a fire when you are not watching.

Glossary

apprentice: a person who works with an experienced person to learn a trade.

atmosphere: the layer of air that surrounds Earth.

backdraft: an explosion that happens when a sleeping fire wakes up suddenly.

conduction: heat moving through a substance.

convection: heat causing air to move in circles.

erupt: to break out suddenly and violently.

extinguisher: a device that sprays foam to put out a fire.

fire gases: gases created when fuel burns.

friction: the rubbing of one thing against another.

ignite: to catch on fire or set on fire.

internal combustion engine: an engine that is powered by a series of small explosions that go off inside it.

lava: hot liquid rock that flows from a volcano.

meteor: an object that burns as it falls through Earth's atmosphere.

meteorite: a meteor that reaches a planet's surface.

meteor shower: many meteors "raining down" in a short period of time.

oxygen: a gas in the air.

phosphorus: a chemical that catches fire and burns easily.

pilot light: a small flame that always burns and is used to relight the main burners in a furnace or fireplace.

radiation: waves of energy, such as heat.

reproduce: create offspring.

Index

Web Sites

volcano.und.nodak.edu/vwdocs/kids/kids.html

www.sparky.org

www.survivealive.org

www.smokeybear.com

Some web sites stay current longer than others. For further web sites, use your search engines to locate the following topics: *fire, firefighting, meteors,* and *volcanoes.*